SNAPSHOTS

EXPLOSIVE POETRY

BRIAN MACKENZIE

Thank you to Mike Hurry for the front cover picture. Who is Mike Hurry? Well that's him behind the camera.

Contents

INTRODUCTION

This is a different collection than my usual output. These are more instant and 'snapshots' that come into my head and I get them down before they disappear. Funny how you get some good ideas when you are having a good drink and listening to music. If you try and remember these ideas the next day, they usually have disappeared. If only we could do a quick 'snapshot' of them, then we could catch them and see them in the cold light of another hangover.

I usually try and think that there is a potential that they can be turned into songs. I have collaborated with Desert Life in the past and hope there are enough ideas here that can be adapted for albums to come.

FROM THE NORTH
so cold

these Scots
so cold
grandfathers fought
the herring shoals
the wild wind
and endless battles
of the seas moods

these Norwegians
so cold
fishermen trolled
the north seas
a little oil
suddenly rich
with the biggest pensions
that's ever been

these souls
from the outer isles
so cold
now see the daily news
did it change their life?
do they still love?
break each other's hearts
or like the grey seals
carry on as they are

IN SEARCH OF GOD

in here you're scum
they serve you food
not fit for a dog in rage
lock down twenty three hours a day
Screws turn a blind eye
you're safer in a lion's cage
they've got you by the balls

you stare deep
into the Devil's eyes
and you'll never see God
inside these walls

these corner boys
hassle out their deals
pimps check their bitch
a tramp looks for a doorway to rest
funny how you found it here
a cop makes out his snitch
alone with no one to meet

you stare deep
into the Devil's eyes
and you'll never see God
out on the street

the stench of fear
is shared by them all
it's over the wall at dawn
whistle blows time to face the Hun
bullets fly all around
friends cut down and gone
the horrors of death revealed

you stare deep
into the Devil's eyes
and you'll never see God
on the battlefield

CICADA'S SONG

a summer love

we loved through the summer heat
listened long to the cicada's song
taste of salt on your darkened skin
we lay close in siesta warmth
kisses fuelled by cupid's reach
shared the wine a chilled Chablis
watch the waves as they rise and fall
like your breasts when you lay with me

the smell of jasmine filled the air
peaches swollen, ripe and sweet
these hazy nights were romantic lit
fireflies and moonbeam lights
touch each other in electric air
so easily I could have died there
we clung together in limpets grip
how night catches dawn is so unfair

but summer ends
and heads to fall
you must return
to a world unreal

don't forget me
in your world out there
every golden memories pain
will last forever
and with me remain

JUST LIKE YOU
the troubles

they've got two eyes
a nose and a mouth
come from the north, west
east and the south
they speak just like you
so why do you hate them?
want to hurt them
kill them
I don't have a clue
if they are kind, honest and true
just like you
does it matter?
if they're Hindu, Catholic, Muslim or Jew

it doesn't seem right
there's no logic to this
it's something I don't understand
you drink the same beer
say hello when you meet
your kids go to the same school
play together in the street
why turn your kids?
to be just like you
living in fear and dread
see their friends go to prison
or end up dead
you've got all this anger and hate
why can't you stop it?
live together in peace
before it's too late

if they are kind, honest and true
just like you
does it matter?
if they're Hindu, Catholic, Muslim or Jew

TO THE WIND

when it's time
for me to go
follow everyone before
i've been caught
with no escape
now I guess i'll have to pay
for all i've sinned

I don't want
some grey old stone
just throw my ashes
to the wind

all your money
all your fame
it don't mean one dam thing
we're all the same
when the Reaper calls
now it's time for you to pay
for all you sinned

when I look back
I might just sigh
I could have been better
that's an honest lie
but what the hell
now it's time for me to pay
for all i've sinned

I don't want
some grey old stone
just throw my ashes
to the wind

MALT

close the curtains
no light
we don't want anybody to see
pour a strong one
it's got to help
the beer is failing me

and if I fall
it's ok
i'm on my own
there's no one here to see

I pour another strong one
plenty ice to make it good
the playlist
all these sad songs
but I guess it's what I need

that line makes me think of you
I almost breakdown
I blame the malt
for my tears
it's not so pure you know

and if I fall
it's ok
i'm on my own
there's no one here to see

SHIFTING SANDS

the sadness that I hold
won't go away
it's found a home to rest
and bound to stay
it doesn't stop me thinking
with memories to the fore
when we flew with the birds
flying high with no care
we opened every door
it doesn't stop me wondering
what happened to it all?
we lost our dreams
got derailed
took our eye of the ball
now i'm locked in reflection
vacant time in my hands
I must accept the rules of play
she's gone with the sullen wind
lost forever in the shifting sands

THE EAGLE SOARS

oh! the glory of the past
rise again terracotta warriors
your tentacles are spreading fast

the great bear released
he wants it back all that's his
who can stop the powerful beast

final battle time to pray
Armageddon for the infidels
prepare now for judgement day

with God's chosen youth
a land of hope and freedom
the eagle soars with all his truth

LIGHT

Shadows dance in the failing light
darkness clings to the longest night
wake in the morning
with the sun behind clouds
all these innocent bodies
covered in shrouds

Hearts that panic at every sound
hide in places that are underground
it's difficult to sleep
covered in torn ragged flags
all these innocent bodies
in black body bags

Sit in a cafe just passing the time
share a bottle of chilled white wine
look up to the sky
see the sun smiling down
feeling happy and safe
with love all around

THE HAPPY SONG

are you happy?
are you happy?
are you happy
with your life?

when you were young
so very young
when innocence was pure
did you think it would be like this
people not always nice
with no smiles in their eye
they can hurt you
say cruel things
and make you cry

when you first met her
sweetest of days
it was a love at first sight
did you think her love was forever?
but she turned away
became distant and cold
shattered dreams
all these lies
a life now on hold

when you were young
so very young
play soldiers with friends
did you think it would be like this?
these guns and bullets
that now kill and maim
when they fall dead
they don't get up
life just a cruel game

no, i'm not happy
i'm not happy
i'm not happy
with this life
i'm not happy with my life

WHERE MY HEART LIES

these feelings that I get
when we take the field
shivers from deep inside
against the odds
we will take them on
our hearts filled with pride

we watch in awe
with these beating hearts
moments remain in time
we will not yield
and will carry on
until we cross the line

oh! to breathe
the fresh Highland air
see the heather hills
forests of tall fir tree
silver snake the river Ness
winding to the sea

JUST A DREAM

we look up and see clear skies
she smiles and takes my hand
people wave as you pass by
hope shines from all their eyes

is this the beginning of a new dawn
now that war is gone

so good to see the children play
free to enjoy their innocence
a future to look forward to
dad is home from being away

is this the beginning of a new dawn
now that war is gone

now we appreciate little things
we've learned what matters
money is not so important
love and kindness and what it brings

is this the beginning of a new dawn
now that war is gone

the wildebeest roam the plains
search where grass is green
they don't need a country
restricted by its border chains
without any countries
there will be no more war

BLESS

oh! it's only dad
he's getting old
always makes stupid mistakes
if only he would leave it
to the ones who know
the professionals
he's getting old

bless!

so I made a mistake
I can't sine in
maybe you put in the wrong code
or forgot

bless!!

don't worry we can do it for you
the professionals
he's getting old
bless!

can you listen
I might be getting old
but I know exactly
what's going on
I can manoeuvre
round any PC or phone
I can't help if their program
is screwed

don't worry we will sort it out for you
he's getting old

bless!

what is left?
when the years catch up

I know they all mean well
give all the love they can
but what is left
when the years catch up
there is only self-respect

bless!!

STRANGERS

she was so bright
full of life and wit
her eyes sharp and blue
now they're grey
filled with sadness
who you are
she hasn't got a clue

is there anything worse than this
you're a stranger now
you don't exist

so full of life
her eyes filled with love
when you were close
she had energy to spare
now her soul
in her lonely cloud
is slowly being squeezed
her eyes now a blank stare

is there anything worse than this
you're a stranger now
you don't exist

ÀLWAYZ

there is no place I can go
nowhere I can hide
if I run, walk or slide
try to swim
against the tide

she's alwayz
on my mind

I can't forget her
she follows me
if i'm on a train
drive a car
or on plane
I know it's sad
and seems insane

but she's alwayz
on my mind

at the top of Mauna Kea
in the darkness underground
wearing earphones
to keep out sound
when l try to find my sleep
she's still around

she's alwayz
on my mind

when i'm with you
in our embrace
I can't help it
but I see her face
so it's best you know
in the early dawn
you could never
take her place

she's alwayz
on my mind

A SILENT THANKS

they're torturing for pleasure
barbaric evil men
killing for any reason
blood lust overflowing
woman used and stoned
what right have they to tell you
how to live your lives
stray from their rigid rules
suffer beatings and torture
all in the name of religion
what kind of a God
would allow this to happen?

Satan he smiles in background
a silent thanks
for his work being done

SHANGHAIED

shanghaied, press ganged
into Her Majesty's Service
a sailor's lot
step out of line
you're over the barrel
feel the lash
a cat o nine tails
or barnacles across your back

rickets and scurvy
the stench of sweat and grime
only thing to look forward to
is another tot of rum
dark and damp
your place to sleep
riddled with rats disease
if you could only
cut the jib and run

the mainsails high
catches the wind
cuts through the enemy lines
master gunner
cannons fire
from deep within the bows
hear the screams
pain and loss of life
i'd rather die
than face a surgeon's knife

hail Horatio
Admiral of the fleet
looks down from high above
with Victory, another battle won
he thanks his men
who cheer and clap
they sing sea shanties

as they drink their extra tots of rum

ALL FOR YOU

you take all that I give
my time you steal away
why do you squeeze my heart
hidden pain you can't see

it's about what you want
you'll pay the price one day

you take all that I have
there's nothing left for me
these dreams I had now gone
you took away my songs

you do not have a clue
the trouble you lay on me
carry on with all your games
your cruel hurtful ways

it's about what you want
you'll pay the price one day

AN EASTER MEMORY

wintertime is gone now
spring is on its way
flowers pushing through
colours from the grey
Happy Easter everyone
little fluffy chicks
bunnies and skipping lambs
chocolate eggs for all the kids
the family gather round
for the feast on Easter day
can you remember
what it's all about?
my memories at a loss
some say a guy called Jesus
died to save us all
they nailed his hands and feet
to a wooden cross
and left him there to die
but apparently, he didn't die

MY FATHERS'

when I think about the past
kept the Romans in England's fields
the marauding Vikings from the north
a strength that never yields
there with Bruce and Wallace heart
he followed blind the young Pretender
to Culloden from the start

I thank my Fathers'
I raise my dram
thanks to them
they got me here

when I think about the past
the famines hardship lives so tough
both great wars the pains they fought
their lives so hard so rough
follow the herring north sea shoals
tilled the land from their little crofts
struggling to fill their bowls

I thank my Fathers'
I raise my dram
thanks to them
they got me here

ANOTHER DEPRESSING SONG

from an uneasy calm
a raging thunderous storm
all I am, everything you hate
the past stirred up
in darkest rolling clouds

should I take this shit
I try to remember your state
your vitriol spiteful words
it's hard not to believe
you don't want me dead

what did I do wrong?
to deserve the hate you give
i'm beginning to lose my faith
it hurts me how you sleep
all your precious life away

ASHES IN A JAR

I never used to worry
or think about a time to die
maybe just a passing thought
it could be about 70
when I started to think about it
quite a lot
maybe for a few seconds
but it's always there
hanging over me
a dark cloud about to rain
one things that's good 'tho
you're not alone
all your movie stars
dudes, dictators
down and outs
they share with you
a casket
or ashes in jar

BATTLE OF LA DRANG
'65

La Drang
valley of death
Huey birds dropped them in
the 7th Cavalry
rookie U.S. soldiers
first time from home
they had to face
the Vietcong
battle hardened
who had already
put the French to sword

in this hot stinking jungle
dead or alive
no American soldier
will be left behind
that's your mate
his head blown off
10,000 miles
from Texas State
you can't stop Charlie
he keeps on coming
from the dark depths
of the earth it seems
get a medic over here
Johnny boy has caught one
give him morphine
if he screams

we got no bullets
running short of body bags
a full moon
in the sky
lights up our dead
we're surrounded
on all flanks
Col Hal tells no lies

they'll attack at dawn
we got no chance
but to hold the line
a flock of birds
sent from heaven
saves our slaughter
blasts these commies
straight to hell

all their bodies
piled high
we could at least
have shown respect
for everyone
who fought and died

SCREAM TO THE DEVIL

scream she will die
from a broken heart
dogs are scared
they pick up the vibe
smothered in stress
the guilt you feel
strain and tension
seems normal now
atmosphere of gloom
is all so real

once again
the bottle wins
fleeting moments
it helps turn it round
then the payback
disgust and regret
for all the time
you tried to steal

if you're not able
to pick yourself up
there is always the devil
go talk to him
and make a deal

CATTLE CLASS

train whistle blows
going to the east
a change of scenery
i'm sure there will be work
out there
travel cattle class
maybe we'll stop for food
and get some relief
things can't be so bad
out there
the journey ends
it was long and cruel
I join the queue
for a welcome shower
they will need our skills
to help the war
things can't be so bad
out here

RIVER FLOW

I look up to the sky
see billions of twinkling stars
mars has a warm red glow
the man in the moon
has a smile on his face
a rainbow in all its colours
tells the rain to go

and as if you didn't know
my love for you
is like the river flow

Bees are buzzing
all over the place
making their honey
that's sweet to taste
birds teach their kids
how to fly from the nest
butterflies dance as they go

and as if you didn't know
my love for you
is like the river flow

I look up and the sky is blue
if you're good and kind
you'll reap what you sow
I love when flowers
are in fullest bloom
it's funny how trees
always wave as you go

and as if you didn't know
my love for you
is like the river flow

BLIND DUTY

can we blame you?
brought up to their lies
you were taught
to hate and despise
follow blindly the leader
whatever the call
die for the fatherland
and proudly fall

what would you do?
caught up in it all
a superior race
intelligent and tall
Europe is taken
in Germany's grip
it's easy to be blind
when you're holding the whip

we were following orders
it's our duty to do
a soldier in battle
will follow what's true
they are the enemy
whoever they are
if we are told to shoot
we fire without any scar

it looks clear to me
it didn't take very much
to turn into killers
humanity losing touch
accepting all evil
when it's good for you
then making lame excuses
for the millions you slew

BLOOMS

all it needs is a little care
some water
make sure
that she's all right
she will tell you
if she's needs
a little more
and if she blooms
you will reap
the kindness that you sow

D DAY

Junho, Amaha, Utah
Gold and Sword
fortified beaches
on Normandy shores
sands of slaughter
the largest seaborne invasion
that ever was
amphibious landing craft
battled strong winds
they came in waves
ever flowing
brave young men
ran on to the beaches
to face their fears
naked and open
to the German rattling guns
blow up by mines
with no place to hide
friends falling
maimed, shot to bits
this for victory
on D day
the beginning of the end
of Nazi rule
and to liberate France
and end that sickening war

DOLPHINS

every day they gently
break the waves
dolphins
perfectly live
beneath the sea
or do they?
do they suffer?
like we do
do they fall out of love?
do dolphins love?
do they suffer?
like you and me

EASE YOUR SOUL

you took everything
you could steal
with no regards for others
you used them all
without any feeling
but it took its toll
when you saw the hurt
you've done
a thief who needs redemption
with conscience that is reeling
there was no guilt
that lingered
always looking for a scam
to rip them off
it didn't seem real
stole what they had
with all their pain
you shrugged
always turned away believing
weakness was theirs to steal
was it a light you saw
some dream
but something hit hard
no going back
just your regret
why were you so cruel?
you made no excuse
but greed
now you can't sleep a wink at night
deserving everything that you get

ETERNAL PEACE

no more breakups
no more pain
say goodbye
to hypocrites
thieves and cheats

no more money worries
no more bad dreams
say goodbye
to cancer
guns and knives

no more broken hearts
no more trolls
say goodbye
to murder
lies and deceit

say hello to happiness
eternal peace

no more anger
no more Jihad
say goodbye
to sadness
bombs and war

no more depression
no more evil
say goodbye
to jealousy
terror and disease

no more slavery
no more rape
say goodbye
to suffering
religion and stress

say hello to happiness
eternal peace

I THINK OF HER

I wonder does she thinks of me
i'm lost in thoughts about her
if she ever feels that she is cold
I will wrap her save in warmest fur
if she ever feels that she is sad
I will gather up and sweep away
all these things that make it bad

I wonder does she think of me
all my senses she does ignite
if she ever feels that she's alone
I will put my arms around her tight
if she ever feels that she is down
I will be the jester make her laugh
playing the fool a sad old clown

I wonder does she thinks of me
sweetest girl I've ever known
if she ever feels that she is lost
I'll take her hand bring her home
if she decides she wants to stray
then my heart it will break in two
all my colours will turn to grey

MY DOG

so sweet my dog
he sees through the hurt
his eyes go sadly dark
he don't need the shouting
the angry words
that strangle around
he wants the couch
his peace and comfort
after the strain
of a perfect walk
why should he suffer
darkness endure
my dog
you deserve my love
and more

ALL THAT WAS TRUE

I wake in the night
and turn to hold you
I panic, then remember
that you're gone
I lie awake in the darkness
until light of the dawn

hopelessly in love
I can't help how I feel
what once was my heart
is now shattered
you were all that I wanted
everything I desired

living in false hope
that you'll come back
this loneliness that I feel
to pass each day
the pain that I now suffer
will never go away

you can't make someone love you
so I will try and hold on
to all that was true

REMINICE

it’s not been all bad
mostly good times too
remember our silly dreams
when we get old
we could hold hands along the beach
and reminisce

well I guess we got there
fifty years against the odds
me from the cold cold north
you a beauty from the warm hot south
I would love if we could share
these twilight times
beautiful glorious
golden sunshine’s
maybe in Phi Phi or Bali
Inverness or Nice
or anywhere!
theses twilight times we can share
we could hold hands along the beach
and reminisce

OXYGEN

don't tell me it's over
I can’t breathe
these things you say
come from a storm
a raging tempest
of hail and rain
just dark clouds
that can lift
I can’t breathe
you say you don't love me
I can’t breathe
you tell me it’s over
I can’t breathe
I need oxygen
I can’t breathe
without you

PASSOVER

it's so cruel
sitting next to you
I can feel your heat
smell your hair
I can't tell you
that I love you
it would spoil what is there
you might look at me
and stare
turn and walk away

but I know
you wouldn't
hurt me
you would let me down slow
but it's best
I keep my thoughts
to myself
my dreams intact
maybe one day
you will look at me
love light in your eyes
so I will
live in hope
I could not face
another day
if you turned
and walked away

PAT'S BAR

women weep in sorrow
at distorted faces
Taliban fighters in gluts
queue to marry tiny young virgins
things don't change
only new faces
at Pat's Bar

the yellow peril is here
it crept in so slow
history just turns its head
put your hands before your eyes
it may just go away
everything's clear
at Pat's Bar

it all feels so normal
almost peaceful
a pterodactyl swoops
the general dragged of screaming
Hemingway claps
as the bell tolls
for Pat's Bar

SHE IGNITES

when I see her
she gives me shivers
I just want to hold her tight
kiss her lips
caress her hair
all my passion
she ignites

these butterflies
that turn inside
my tongue gets tied
with no place to hide

do you believe
in loves first sight?
I didn't before
but now I might

all threw the day
into the night
she's always there
I just can't fight

dare to tell her
I'm tied in knots
I love you babe
she loves me lots

I believe
in loves first sight
we lie together
all through the night

will my love last forever
who knows what will be
but now it's good
that's enough for me

when I see her
she gives me shivers
I just want to hold her tight
kiss her lips
caress her hair
all my passion
she ignites

SIGNAL BOX

start your journey
board the train
travel in hope
wherever it goes
different places
sometimes lost
just go how it flows

stop at a station
meet new friends
some are kind
others let you down
your baggage
gets off
left behind

moving along
different places
changing scenes
mountains, hills
jungles, forests
rivers and streams

chugging along
picking up speed
to your journeys end

people get off
new ones get on
it's sad to lose
good old friends
along the line
another stop
but it's not the end

bad weather ahead
dark clouds and rain
rainbows brings

blue skies again

a crowded carriage
laughter and love
now on your own
things are calm
faster and faster
at blinding speed
keep on the track
one last bend
it's time to get off
at your journeys end
at the station
no one to meet
waiting there
no one to love
not even a friend
there must be a hostel
a place to go

SMARTIES

it's the day she been waiting for
time to pick up her smarties
it's so good when she runs out
at least I see her in the evenings
things are almost normal
almost normal
well normal for me

it's my worst days
when she gets her smarties

into perma sleep now
until her coloured friends run out
moments awake in slurred speech
the vitriol starts
that she won't remember
I struggle to get her to eat

it's my worst days
when she gets her smarties

another anniversary missed
slept it through
guess I'll drink on my own
any excuse to celebrate
celebrate
just have to wait
until the smarties are gone
then things get back to almost normal
almost normal
we'll normal for me

it's my worst days
when she gets her smarties

SPHERE

when it's dark
beyond the light
shadows creep slow
the air is heavy
it strangles
the lamp light glow
every rustle
increases your fear
a horrid dread
cramps your guts
whatever it is
drawing near
creeping closer
ever closer
an evil stench
brings its danger
invades your sphere
nothing you can feel
is clear
clutching a crucifix
you curl up
pray it's a dream
bile rising
panic becomes a scream

TELL ME I'M NOT

don't put me down
when I'm trying to be happy
don't put me down
when all I want, is to listen
to a little good music
don't tell me I'm bad
when I don't share your pain

I know you won't listen
if I say i'm on your side
if only I can help
am I the bad guy

tell me I'm not

don't throw it away
use every second that is left
if you need, forget about me
be the girl that I love
what do I know about
the sadness of lost minds?

I wake in the morning
hangover blue
I hear the Burning Spear
from last night
every day I try to lift myself
worrying about you
i'm on your side
am I the bad guy

please tell me I'm not

ON A PLANE

sometimes we go far
to earn our way
no matter what it takes
but it comes at such a cost
we leave behind our family and friends
sometimes the girl we love

is there anything better
than being on a plane
going home to the ones you love

I feel for the workers
who've got no choice
they come from the east
and worked too hard
living in conditions
not fit for a dog
just to keep their families alive
their strife we will never understand
it is sometimes years
before they see their sons
I cry at the injustice that's done

is there anything better
than being on a plane
going home to the ones they love

I still get excited
to be going home
to see and hug them close
why have we got to be away from them all?
why is life so shit sometimes?

is there anything better
than being on a plane
going home to the ones you love

TORRETA
a romantic view

to be here in Salino
where white doves fly
protected by
walls of green trees
you can hear
the joyous sounds
of children at play
the gentle woofs!
of man's best friends
sit on the terraces
of Chi Chi Poon
be witness to brilliant sunsets
of orange glow
the red lake shimmers
as the sun goes down
magnificent pyramids
of pure white gold
rest your weary bones
at Patricia's place
where minstrels and jokers play

YOU ARE INVINCIBLE

'I have confidence
in all the sensible British people'
my ass
get ready for lockdown
get ready for anarchy
get ready for economic collapse

social distance my friends
go out to the rave
party with your mates
stay close in the pub
hug and kiss
you are invincible

go home
infect you mum
your sister and dad
kill your Nan
you are invincible

get ready for lockdown
get ready for anarchy
get ready for economic collapse

A FLEETING GLANCE

can I still run a marathon
even although my feet are bad
climb to the top of Kilimanjaro
jungle to artic snow
who knows the time you have left?
each day you should use to the full
but I use my time looking after you
with happiness
because that's what you would do for me
I steal a drink here and there
a nod to acquaintances known
only staying until my seat
doesn't get too warm
sometimes a fleeting glance
and the guilt that I then feel

THE GREATEST GIFT

what's it like in perma sleep?
like bears and squirrels
who sleep the winter through
do you dream, see colours?
or is like when you're sent to sleep
under the surgeon's knife
is it like before you were born?
nothing to remember
your perma sleep
away from the world
its beauty and shit
do you not care anymore?
the pain you put
your love ones through
squandering the minutes and seconds
of the greatest gift of all

IT'S JUST THE SUNSHINE

there goes our song
the one we used to sing
before you said goodbyes
it's not real tears
that you see
it's just the sunshine
in my eyes

do you remember when
we used to skip along
stars twinkled in the skies
when we didn't even have to try
when you looked deep into my eyes
love came to us as no surprise
these days were pure with no need for lies
never lows but only highs
a love forever that never dies

there goes our song
the one we used to sing
before you said goodbyes
it's not real tears
that you see
it's just the sunshine
in my eyes

80 YEARS A TRAVELIN'

happy 80th birthday Bob
it's be a long time traveling
a troubadour
going round the world
giving us your songs
it's a never ending trail
your voice maybe a little broken
but the message still strong
i've been with you
since 64
bootlegs and concerts
the hidden gems
the Beatles and Elvis you can't fault
but you Bob are the greatest
of them all

NOTHING WILL EVER CHANGE

They called us up
we had to go
they shoot deserters
you'd better know
they trained us up
showed us ways
how to kill a man
a man the same as me
we've got no choice
but have to fight
or else we can´t be free
sent to the front
a hellish place
no man should ever see
mud and blood
cold and damp
over the wall
to face their bullets
at the whistle call
running blind
screaming men
flesh ripped apart
blow to bits
my dearest friends
crawl back home
with the stench of fear
to do it all again
millions lost for nothing
loved ones left behind
after all the carnage
what was the point of it all
nothing will ever change

WHERE WAS I

I only tell it how it is
never ever self-pity
with no right to deserve
always at the back of my head
I think of them all
who suffered
tortured, abused
where was I
when they cried for help

I only tell it how I feel
with maybe no rights
I would never consider
that I need or deserve any help
when I look at the world
the sadness and pain
that others go through
my sad little world
is nothing to compare
where was I
when they cried for help

WE CRY

that’s our mum
trying her best
to be who she was
we scream to ourselves
that we can't help her any more
after what she's done for us all

we pretend
it's like it was
moments that shine through
how it used to be
she took the lead
led us there
she was everyone's girl
she was our mum
the life and soul

now she's slow
doesn't understand
so well
trying hard
to be who she was
all our tears fall down
if only she can find her sleep
tonight
find some peace
in herself

WILL YOU EVER KNOW

oh! these flowers that you choose
is it because of brilliant blooms?
or because of subtle colours and leaves
but will you ever know what they want?
to keep them alive and full of life
loving care and tenderness
a special soil with all their needs

how you want to own that orchid
with her colours in full display
if she can hold all that gorgeous beauty
but will you ever know what she wants?
maybe she needs just a little water
please don't smother her
or she may die and wither away

KRAKEN

where did it come from
hidden somewhere deep
from the dark shadows
caught off guard
she strikes with no remorse
gorging on the juices of love
leaving a hollow empty carcass
throw to the wind

sweetest mermaid
flowing golden hair
her mystery, her kindness
a gift from the ocean
she enchants
as she takes over your heart
your life in a spin
but she is restless
when you gave her your soul
her anger arises
true colors, she changes
an evil Kraken
behind her fair skin

caught off guard
she strikes with no remorse
gorging on the juices of love
leaving a hollow empty carcass
throw to the wind

COCOON

it feels so safe and warm
doors and windows closed
it keeps out the cold and rain
I don't feel naked and exposed

most people I believe are kind
but here, no one's going to hurt me
i'm safe in my cocoon

why should I go out there?
when I can't trust a single soul
I know everyone is not so bad
but here at least I have control

I know I must try my best
my fear, no confidence is real
the outside world I must re-join
pick myself up and start to heal

most people I believe are kind
but here no one's going to hurt me
i'm safe in my cocoon

if only my sweetheart, my love
if only you'll come home soon

BORN TO TIE

oh! my, oh! my
we don't have to try
it comes so natural
like a lover's knot
we were born to tie

these tears we cry
are happiness
and joy
we are both
way up there
in natural high
all the love
that we supply
gives the strongest knot
that can't untie

sometimes, I wonder why
i'm so lucky
to be with you
the love we have
you cannot buy
it's a lover's knot
we were born to tie

we're way up there
in natural high
oh! my, oh! my
we don't have to try
a lover’s knot
that can’t untie

PATH OF THE WIND

wakened from you sleep
the fog at last is clear
all that's been before
everything that you held dear
it was very hard to learn
who you truly are
you're not who you thought you were
you weren't even near

these so called friends
they've fallen through
its better to be alone
no one to disappoint you
don't trust these words
they spit from their mouths
they can and twist the truth
and say things that are not true

when you lie close to her
it's a desolate cruel place to be
your silent screams
keeps you awake at nights
so don't be seeking any new loves
it's just cruelty to your heart
just follow the path of the wind
it's a safer place to be

COCKTAILS OF LOVE

Primroses, snowdrops and dandelion tears
lilies, roses and cherry blossom bloom
orchids, violets and snowdrops in spring
dalia's, magnolias and red lotus flower

Blend them together
in a cocktail of love
we raise our glass high to the lord above
and drink a celebration
to the perfection of our love

Puppies, kittens and skipping spring lambs
ducklings, cubs and pretty Easter chicks
pandas, koalas and doe eyed fawns
hamsters, white mice and birds of paradise

Blend them together
in a cocktail of love
we raise our glass high to the lord above
and drink a celebration
to the happiness of our love

Lobster, salmon and southern fried chicken
curry, chop suey and rare Argentine steak
champagne, caviar and smoky pure malt
chocolate, ice cream and French apple pie

Blend them together
In a cocktail of love
we raise our glass high to the Lord above
and drink a celebration
to the tastes of our love

Bithworts, corpse flowers and stinky squid thorn
hemlock, nightshade and white snake root
monkshood, rosary peas and thorn of the cross
dracunculus vulgaris and eastern skunk cabbage

Blend them together
in a cocktail of love
we raise our glass high to Satan below
and drink a celebration
to the carcass of our love

Vipers, fruit bats and nightstalkers that sting
spiders, dung beetles and salties that prey
piranhas, tigers and biting great whites
mosquitoes, box jelly fish and poison dart frogs

Blend them together
in a cocktail of love
we raise our glass high to Satan below
and drink a celebration
to the entrails of our love

Fish eyes, pig's guts and sewerage that smells
road kill, rotten eggs and witchity grubs
puss, gangrene and steaming fresh vomit
maggots, offal and putrid old corpse

Blend them together
in a cocktail of love
we raise our glass high to Satan below
and drink a celebration
to the carrion of our love

INTERSTELLER

came from an interstellar jet stream
riding down the solar wind
firing pulsar neutron blasts
we didn't stand a chance
they caught us off our guard
came from a spiralling super cluster
faster than the speed of light
firing quantum lascr waves
caught without defences
we didn't see them come
within Andromeda's celestial sphere
down and past Orion's sword
firing invisible gamma rays
the few that were left
had to find ourselves a plan

SOLID STONE EIGHT

we passed by Jimmy's place
bright lights and flashing sign
heading down to Sharky’s pool
on my game, I hit the money ball
Billy dogged the nine

tonight's the night of green bay
a big game at the Golden Rush
fold if you think you’re in too deep
cards are dealt, three of a kind
Billy turns a Royal Flush

down again at Sharky’s pool
I was set up and took the bait
don’t bet if you can’t take the heat
me I had to ride the lightning
Billy on solid stone eight

BLINDNESS

why can't you see?
she doesn't want you anymore
she wants to spread her wings
escape from the cage
you keep her in

why can't you see?
it's over
she has gone to the arms
of her lover
leaving you with memories
you don't want to let go

why can't you see?
with your pathetic sad hope
that she'll drop everything
and come running back
you can't work it out
that you don't break someone's heart
if you love them

why can't you see?
it's over

IN THE LINE OF DUTY

I gave you everything that you needed
worked hard to give you what you want
a brand new kitchen, a Dyson ball
holidays in the sun
always had flowers on your special days
chocolates for your birthday
I thought I gave you it all

how could you possibly have left me
I did everything by the book
in the line of duty

I never needed to stay out late at night
worked hard always around the house
I picked you up if you had a fall
I was always there
held your hand going down the street
always opened doors for you
I thought I gave you it all

how could you possibly have left me
I did everything by the book
in the line of duty

THE GUILT I FEEL

will never go

got no friends
no one to talk to
nobody to like me
or think i'm special
only you to put me down

how could anybody like me
i'm useless
all my thoughts too dark
and my stupid poetry
a peasant from the north
nobody could ever love me

got no friends
i'm not allowed to
how can I enjoy myself?
when you can't
it would be so unfair
and uncaring
if you are ill and depressed
I must be too?

no more guilt
no more tearing my hair out
I have to have a life you know

then I get more guilt
when you don't understand things
don't understand the movie
forget things
I feel guilt when I shout
when you don't understand

got no friends
no one to talk to
the guilt I feel

will never go

WHITE SKIN

because of the past
all you've been taught
now feel the wrath
of the yellow waves
do you think it's forgotten?
all that you did
a trader in slaves
believe in your own salvation
do you think it's forgotten?
when you've decimated
10,000 years
sent them to rot
in a reservation
it's another lynching
in a Southern state
will it ever be banned?
it's never too late
wiped out the Aztecs
stole all their gold
the glorious Raj
two hundred million in chains
is there anywhere
you haven't destroyed
for your gains
do you think it's forgotten?
do you think it's gone away?

so it's not your fault
who are your kin
but nobody likes you
if you're born with white skin

ONCE WAS A PLAYER

for Trev

after all
where are you now
3 failed marriages
kids you don't know
now in a bed sit
always drinks in the afternoon
with the same old losers
before TV dinner
or takeaway

is this how you've ended
when we all remembered
how you lit up the room
turned them all on
funny and smart
you lit up the room

alone with your losers
you now have the time to fear
desolate and lonely
you only get back
what you give
but I fear it's too late

I feel this sadness
that you've learned too late
but I will happily share
a drink when we next meet

CONSTANT SORROW

how can I be happy
a sense of wellbeing
when you are sad

how can I be happy
in all this gloom
how can I be happy
when you steal
the light from the room

how can I be happy
a sense of wellbeing
when you are sad

how can I be happy
when you don't listen to what I say
how can I be happy
when you turn away
how can I be happy
when I know you are down
how can I be happy
when you don't smile, you only frown
how can I be happy
when you sleep all day
how can I be happy
when there's nothing kind you say
how can I be happy
when I don't know what to do
how can I be happy
when I can't seem to give any help you
how can I be happy
when I hear you cry

how can I be happy
a sense of wellbeing
when you are sad

how can I be happy

when I drink all the time
how can I be happy
when I drink everyday

how can I be happy
a sense of wellbeing
when you say I'm bad

how can I be happy
when I'm bad
how can I be happy
when I’m sad

SANTA'S BEEN EATEN BY SPIDERS

Mummy, daddy
quick come look
Santa's been eaten by spiders
all that's left
is his red velvet coat
can I open my presents please

oh! my boy
Santa's ok
he just left his coat
for mummy to wash

he's snoring in bed
with a big soar head
he drank all the sherry
ate all the cake
I so wish he was eaten
by spiders instead
the fat lazy git

THE SUN WENT DOWN
with apologies to George Harrison

this winter's day with sky blue
you sparkled like the happy sea
this is how it used to be
we held hands by the shore

everything so bright and clear
hold me close look in my eyes
this is how it used to be
we could love forever more

but the sun went down
behind the clouds
it turned cold
and left us there

the sun is high
along the beach
hand in hand
we find a bar
a cool beer
palms sway
white sands shimmer
azure sea cools the shore
we smile and laugh
two more beers
that's how it used to be

but the sun went down
behind the clouds
it turned cold
and left us there

SHADES OF BLUE

Since you've gone
it's all gone wrong
this feeling bad
ain't nothing new
all my colours
they're shades of blue

I never thought
i'd feel this way
my guts they grip
and twist all day
I can't get up
to go to work
I mope about
with head in cloud
the love I had
now wrapped in shroud

this feeling bad
ain't nothing new
all my colours
are shades of blue

they say that love
is the greatest thing
with all the joy
that it can bring
with each day
you can't help but smile
everything you do
all seems worthwhile

but when it all goes wrong
and when she's gone
then feeling bad
ain't nothing new
with all your colours

INSIDE THE WALLS OF ATTICA

Inside the walls of Attica
it's hell to be
do you know what there're in for?
rapists, killers, paedophiles and thieves
they're not human
a man is not a man
inside these walls
he's treated like a dog
it's a time bomb
waiting to explode
ready to burn
inside the walls of Attica

violence with violence
it's all they understand
don't show any kindness
it's a sign of weakness

all we want is decent food
a little respect
basic human rights
so we can do our time
but if you won't let us live like men
we'll tell you this
we can sure as hell
die like men
they were warned it was coming down
but they didn't listen
violence and blood
death and torture
we got control
with their screws as hostage
made our demands
a promise of no revenge
no violence
no repercussions
they promised much
but after 4 days

the bastards opened fire
didn't care who they killed
wardens or inmates

43 dead, massacred cut down
blood flowed like the Niagara falls
inside the walls of Attica

things have got to change
inside the walls of Attica

HOMAGE

she always took her bag to the loo
it contained her half bottle
she was always topped up, just enough
If she went out to the pub
she acted drunk after the first drink
I should have knew

how can I advise anyone not to drink
when I drink more than they do

the drink caught up with her
stole her away
liver shot
taken far too young
liver shot
another victim of alcohol abuse
another addict gone

and I never helped my little sister
I let it happen
even encouraged her to drink
I turned away

did I learn? from this
only nothing
because I choose to
do I still drink
of course I do
am I an alcoholic
yes I am
my sick sad homage to you
regrets
just a few
just a few

REMINICE

it’s not been all bad
mostly good times too
remember our silly dreams
when we get old
we could hold hands along the beach
and reminisce

well I guess we got there
fifty years against the odds
me from the cold cold North
you a beauty from the warm hot south

I would love if we could share
these twilight times
beautiful glorious
golden sunshine’s
maybe in Phi Phi or Bali
Inverness or Nice
or anywhere
theses twilight times we can share

we could hold hands along the beach
and reminisce

WHO WANTS TO GO TO WAR?

who wants to go to war?
fire a gun, shoot to kill
who wants to go to war?
catch a bullet
end up dead
would you rather
be in her arms?
Sunday lunch round at mums
who wants to go to war?

we don't want to have a war
they fire rockets
drop their bombs
destroy our homes
kill our kids
we would rather hold our men
not live in fear
with our future lost
we don't want to have a war

only one man starts a war
steals our lands
steals our lives
he doesn't care what soldiers die
only one man starts a war
to satisfy his ego large
just because he thinks he's God
only one man starts a war

HIGHLIGHTS
in lockdown

panic attacks in the night
you wake in the morning
struggle to get out of bed
put the coffee on
let the dogs out
watch the news
it's lockdown
nothing's going to change
nowhere to go
no one to meet
breakfast, the same old
you wait until you feel
it's ok to have a drink
nothing's coming through
so nothing to write
music won't help
until that first one
you mope about
every little chore
seems hard to do
even the weather's turned
let you down
take the dogs out
no one about
go down to the lakes
it's a highlight
what to eat?
who cares?
time for a drink
the highlight
highlight of the day
at least for a time
fell asleep
missed the end of the movie
panic attacks in the night

COLD STONE SOBER

i'm cold stone sober
heading for the bar
happy hour starting
it's two for one
Jack Daniels neat
heavy on the rocks
followed by a beer
Milwaukee malt

i'm cold stone sober
sitting at the bar
i'm still not happy
and its two for one
Dalmore Malt
heavy on the rocks
followed by a beer
Stella's soon done

i'm cold stone sober
looking round the bar
room's closing in
it's one for one
Crystal Head shot
heavy on the rocks
need more chase
San Miguel's run

not so cold sober
the high's going down
still can't forget you
what went wrong?
Barti Ddu Rum
heavy on the rocks
need another beer
Super Skol strong

SOME CANCER GROW

I don't know when I lost my way
feelings of no confidence
this fear you had given up
your love for me
and wanted to go
but wouldn't say

it was like some cancer grow
in this love
that's lost its way

you weren't there to take my call
maybe I misread the sign
this fear you're with someone else
your love for me
inside his arms
made me feel so small

it was just like some cancer grow
in this love
that consumed my all

because I saw through clouded eyes
with suspicion and jealousy
I spoiled our love that was so good
it wasn't her
who destroyed our love
but me searching for any lies

it was like some cancer grow
in this love
that ended in my demise

SOFT BROWN EYES

with soft brown eyes
that show love and kindness
trust
don't let them down
give a little back
be there for them

they don't ask for much
a little walk
a clap, a cuddle
that's all they want
and to be close to you

we made them
what they are
so don't let them down
always there
when you return
waggy tails
to spoil you
always giving more
than they get
be there for them
they won't let you down

EVEN THE DEVIL WILL LOOK AWAY

How can we smile?
how can we laugh anymore?
just feel the guilt
with the things we look forward to
wake up in panic and fear
it's always there
the threat of Armageddon
images of burning buildings
and destruction
colonies of tanks and rocket launchers
thousands now homeless
on the run
kids without their fathers
old folks
faithful pets left behind

what kind of monster
does this?
even the devil will look away

all the lies they spawn
propaganda to fool his people
Ukraine is a threat to Mother Russian
America, like Hitler and Napoleon
controls all of Europe
paranoia, pathetic justification
for his war machine
and Empire expansion
he doesn't care who he kills

what kind of monster
does this?
even the devil will look away

THE END GAME

you're out in the cold
we hope you freeze
nobody likes you
everyone hates you
they all want you gone
you will never be let back in
your so-called friends
are scared what you'll do
fall from a height
or be poisoned to death
your heart is made of stone
nobody likes you
everyone hates you
there is only one way
it will end

IN PERFECT LOUD

there's a break
up in the clouds
looks like rain
will finally stop
no more bullets
or bombs
will hit the ground
you can hear
the buzz of bees
and birds that sing
in perfect loud

ALSO BY BRIAN MACKENZIE

PAINTED LADIES
a bevy of poetry
Brian Mackenzie

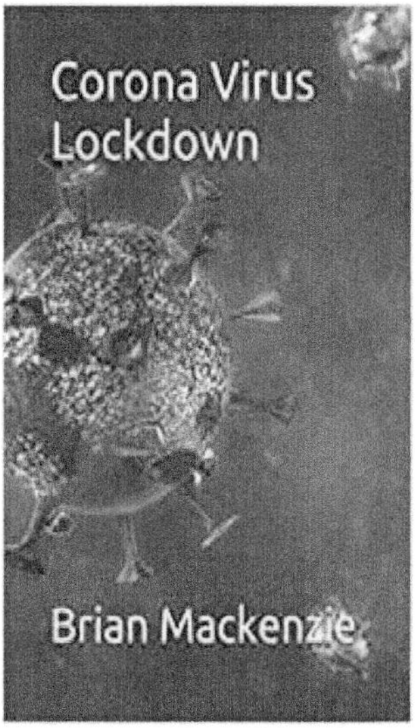
Corona Virus
Lockdown
Brian Mackenzie

RETURN OF THE PAINTED
LADIES
A BEVY OF POETRY
BRIAN MACKENZIE

A ROSE CALLED BARRY
Poetry of Love
BRIAN MACKENZIE

Printed in Great Britain
by Amazon

79402202R00062